WE
Who Believe
in Freedom

T0033366

WE

Who Believe in Freedom

The Life and Times of
Ella Baker

True Tales for Young Readers

No. 2

Lea E. Williams

First Revised Edition, First Printing, 2019

ISBN 978-0-86526-488-5

FRONT COVER: The cover portrait is provided courtesy of the artist Robert Shetterly and the organization Americans Who Tell the Truth (www.americanswhotellthetruth.org), which creates educational opportunities around Shetterly's portraits of courageous citizens.

FRONTISPIECE: Ella Baker in Atlantic City, N.J., site of the 1964 Democratic National Convention, August 10, 1964. *Credit:* The Image Works

BACK COVER: SNCC promotional literature depicted the interracial nature of the group. *Credit:* Shaw University.

Cover and Interior Design: Sheilah Barrett Carroll

The book interior is Minion Pro. The display typefaces are ITC Bradley Hand and Franklin Gothic Family.

Distributed by the University of North Carolina Press, Inc.
www.uncpress.org

In the spirit of fundi and the celebration of Ella Baker's life

True Tales for Young Readers

Contents

Foreword

Narratives such as *We Who Believe in Freedom* are an important way to open ourselves up to the human experience. They provide us with the means to understand our world. Biography, a special form of narrative, allows us to access a singular life. With Lea E. Williams's biography of Ella Baker, we have the opportunity to learn about an extraordinary woman from North Carolina who helped change the world for the better. It is fitting that Williams, who spent time as an administrator at Bennett College in Greensboro, North Carolina, among her other accomplishments, tells this story.

The North Carolina African American Heritage Commission appreciates the work of Lea Williams in bringing attention to the incredible life and work of one of our own African American "sheroes" and daughter of the Tar Heel State—Ella Baker. After reading the story of Ella Baker, you will know why the a cappella group Sweet Honey in the Rock penned "Ella's Song" with the chorus "We who believe in freedom cannot rest."

Valerie Ann Johnson

Dr. Johnson is chair of the North Carolina African American Heritage Commission and Mott Distinguished Professor of Women's Studies/Director of Africana Women's Studies at Bennett College.

Preface

The title *We Who Believe in Freedom* is taken from a speech delivered by Ella Baker in 1964. In it, she said:

> *Until the killing of black men, black mothers' sons,*
> *becomes as important to the rest of the country as*
> *the killing of a white mother's son, we who believe in*
> *freedom cannot rest.*

Bernice Johnson Reagon, a singer, composer, social activist, and founder of the a cappella group Sweet Honey in the Rock, wrote a tribute choral piece titled "Ella's Song" and used those words as the refrain. During her years of civil rights activism, Reagon witnessed firsthand Ella Baker's work in the field. She beautifully captured Baker's spirit of social justice in the song.

According to the Ella Baker Center for Human Rights in Oakland, California, "Ella's Song" "is an anthem, a meditation on the ultimate lesson of the freedom fight passed down generationally by Ms. Ella herself."[1]

Acknowledgments

I have long aspired to acquaint younger readers with the lives of civil rights leaders, especially the lives of women like Ella Baker. Until recently, women activists in the movement remained in the shadows, their stories of courage and behind-the-scenes leadership overlooked and untold. Now, younger audiences can read about the inspiring life of Ella Baker, one of the sharpest minds and most vital community organizers in the civil rights movement.

The assistance of several individuals made this book a reality. Early on, I talked with Tammy Miller, the Youth Services Coordinator at the Greensboro Public Library. She helped me understand the kind of literature that would appeal to young people. Sherry Poole Clark, a graphic designer, looked over the manuscript and made helpful suggestions about the photographs and images. A special appreciation to Howard Gaither, the photographer who immediately responded to my request for a photograph of the Greensboro Four statue on the campus of North Carolina A&T State University. I owe a special nod of appreciation to Michael Hill, Susan Trimble, and Sheilah Barrett Carroll in the North Carolina Office of Archives and History, who coordinated the editing and design. Finally, thanks to all who took an interest in this project and encouraged my efforts.

Introduction

Ella Josephine Baker was fifty-six years old when four freshmen from North Carolina Agricultural and Technical (A&T) College sat down at the whites-only Woolworth lunch counter in downtown Greensboro, North Carolina, ordered coffee, and were refused service. The date was February 1, 1960. Over the next several weeks and months, Ella Baker watched as sit-ins spread throughout the South. With her considerable knowledge of protest movements, she instinctively sensed that these spontaneous acts of civil disobedience had tremendous potential and had ignited

On February 1, 1960, four young men from North Carolina Agricultural and Technical College sat down at a "whites-only" Woolworth lunch counter in Greensboro, North Carolina, and waited to be served. For that time, such action was unprecedented. Ella Baker developed many relationships with college students in the South and helped them organize youth-led peaceful protests.
Credit: Greensboro News and Record

the fires of youth-led protest. The relationship that developed between Baker and the students was one of the most gratifying of her life.

In the years before the sit-ins, Baker had acquired a national reputation in civil rights circles as an expert in community organizing. In fact, colleagues said that she was the most capable organizer in the movement. Since she had expertise to offer, she invited the sit-in student leaders to a conference to discover more about them and the kind of help they might need.

While the initial victories had animated the sit-in leaders, it was obvious to Baker that they were new to leading mass-action campaigns. Not only were the students politically naïve, the majority were uninformed about the underlying historical and philosophical foundations of social justice movements. They also lacked the financial and technical resources needed, over the long haul, to sustain momentum.

However, with Baker's assistance and encouragement, the students formed their own independent organization and named it the Student Nonviolent Coordinating Committee (SNCC), pronounced "snick." In addition to becoming a mentor, friend, and trusted advisor to the group, Baker also helped with logistics. She secured office space and recruited talented staff from her wide circle of movement contacts. Without her connections, her protective advocacy, and her steadying hand, SNCC would have floundered.

Over the course of her decades of fighting for civil rights, Ella Baker enriched the lives of Harlem, New York, youth through public library programs, coordinated major membership campaigns for the National Association for the Advancement of Colored People (NAACP), and helped launch the Southern Christian Leadership Conference (SCLC) after the jubilant victory of the Montgomery, Alabama, bus boycott in 1956.

Baker had a genius and special gift for getting ordinary people to achieve extraordinary deeds. Leadership training was fundamental to her method, as was empowering

hardworking, everyday folks—many with little education and no formal leadership experience— to fight for their rights at the risk of bodily harm, swift reprisals, and violent retribution from whites. Offering training opportunities was how Baker embedded expertise in communities and in organizations. This community-based expertise could grow, become firmly

Ella Baker in the 1940s.
Credit: Library of Congress

established, and reside locally long after Baker and other movement volunteers had left.

Molded by her southern background, bathed in strong Baptist teachings, groomed for leadership at black schools, and tested by movement organizations, Ella Baker became a legendary behind-the-scenes figure during the civil rights movement. Joanne Grant, a SNCC volunteer who produced the documentary film *Fundi: The Story of Ella Baker*,[2] said that "Miss Baker's contributions to the Movement were on a grand scale."[3] Who was Ella Josephine Baker, the legendary civil rights organizer and "godmother of SNCC"?[4]

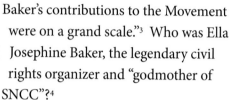

Growing Up in the South

In 1896, Ella Baker's parents, Blake Baker and Georgianna (Anna) Ross Baker, settled in Norfolk, Virginia, as newlyweds and started their family. Ella was born there in 1903. Both Blake and Anna had grown up in rural North Carolina near one another. Blake grew up in Elams, a small community in Warren County, and Anna in Littleton, a town about ten miles from the Virginia border with just over a thousand residents in 1910.

A thriving port town, Norfolk attracted the young couple because it offered better job prospects for Blake. In fact, Blake had relocated to Norfolk before he married and found a job working as a waiter for a steamship company. Once married, Anna joined Blake. She had previously taught school in Littleton but stayed home in Norfolk to raise their children and tend house.

After two unsuccessful pregnancies, Anna gave birth to a boy named Blake Curtis. Two years later, Ella was born. Two other pregnancies ended in miscarriage or

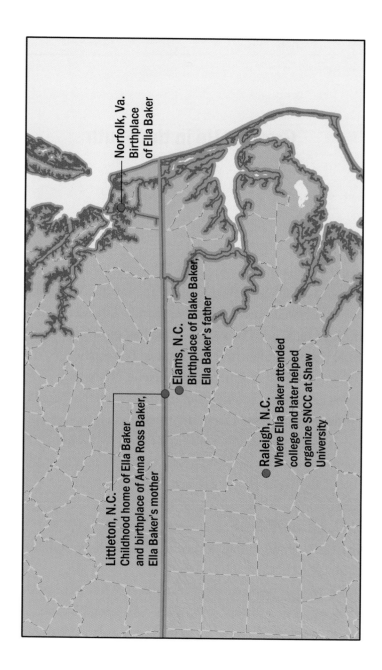

Norfolk, Va.
Birthplace
of Ella Baker

Elams, N.C.
Birthplace of Blake Baker,
Ella Baker's father

Raleigh, N.C.
Where Ella Baker attended
college and later helped
organize SNCC at Shaw
University

Littleton, N.C.
Childhood home of Ella Baker
and birthplace of Anna Ross Baker,
Ella Baker's mother

The railroad depot in Littleton, ca. 1905, with its well-marked segregated waiting rooms. *Credit:* State Archives of North Carolina

stillbirth before Margaret (Maggie) Odessa, the youngest, was born.

When Ella was seven years old, the family moved back to Littleton so that Anna could be closer to her widowed mother. As the eldest daughter, she felt responsible for the care of her aging mother. Ella's father, however, remained in Norfolk to work and commuted to Littleton when he could. Anna was glad to be back home because Norfolk had become more and more racially segregated. Gradually, signs saying "whites only" appeared in public places. Even scarier, a frightening and bloody race riot between whites and African Americans erupted in 1910.

In Littleton, people lived strictly segregated lives in all-white neighborhoods and all-black ones. There were

A business block in Littleton, ca. 1909 (from a postcard).
Credit: State Archives of North Carolina

separate black schools, separate churches, and black-owned businesses. As an adult, Baker recalled that her family "did not come in contact with whites too much."[5] In her close-knit neighborhood, the adults shielded youngsters from many of the ugly incidents that they encountered in the white world.

Through schooling and hard work, Ella's parents moved up the economic ladder in one generation. The family lived comfortably in a rented six-room, two-story house on East End Avenue in Littleton. The nicely furnished house included a formal dining room. The possession of a piano signaled the Bakers' middle-class status.

Many of the adults in the Bakers' section of town had professional or skilled-crafts jobs that allowed them to earn decent incomes. Ella recalled that

South Street Baptist Church in Littleton, N.C., was Ella Baker's home church. The brick veneer was added to the building in the 1940s. *Credit:* N.C. State Historic Preservation Office

Next to us was the Reverend Mr. Hawkins, who, in addition to being a minister, was a bricklayer. And men were artisans like brick plastering and so forth. And somebody else was a carpenter. . . . All of the heads of the families and their wives who lived in the section we called East End were at least literate. They had been to school somewhere, and many of them had been to what might have been considered [a] college or an academy.[6]

Income might have determined where folks lived, but common grievances against racial discrimination created a bond across black neighborhoods. After all, African Americans shopped in the same stores, worshipped at the same churches, attended the same schools, and played in the same segregated parks and recreational facilities. Segregation created a community and made face-to-face encounters between those who had more and those who had less a daily occurrence.

Ella Baker's grandparents lived close by during her childhood and greatly influenced her upbringing. Both sets of grandparents had grown up in slavery. After being freed, however, Anna's parents, Mitchell and Josephine Elizabeth Ross, had the financial resources to purchase a fifty-acre plot of land. According to Baker, they donated a small parcel of this land so that a school could be built for the African American children in the Littleton-Elams area.

As an adult, Ella provided financial assistance to her mother so that she could hold on to the family land, where she had spent summers as a girl. "I suppose the first fifty dollars I made I sent back to help pay taxes on that land because my mother was the only member of her family that sort of kept holding on to it."[7]

Ella fondly remembered her grandfather Ross, who died when she was around six or seven. In the few years they had together, he doted on her, encouraged her endless curiosity, and enjoyed listening to her surprisingly grown-up conversations.

That same curiosity had the opposite effect on her mother; it frequently taxed her nerves. Ella recalled a favorite childhood story that happened in Norfolk and outraged her mother. One day, as a gentleman who lived down the street passed by, Ella asked if he would be her godfather.

He answered and wanted to know why. I said, "Because you're so nice and black, like my grandfather." And he agreed, but of course it turned out that he was a Presbyterian. And my mother, who was a very positive lady, did not think that her father would rest well in his grave if his children or his grandchildren became anything else but Baptists. So that was that.[8]

Everybody in the family knew that Ella was her grandfather Ross's favorite grandchild. His nickname for her was "Grand Lady."[9] Grandfather Ross's loving attention made Ella feel special as a child and built a self-confidence that she carried into adulthood.

Ella's father's parents, Teema and Margaret Baker, had a very different and not-so-prosperous life story. Because neither could read or write, they had few options for earning a living after emancipation. They remained on the slave plantation and rented a parcel of land to farm as tenants. In theory, tenant farmers were more independent than sharecroppers. They could manage the farming process from start to finish, deciding what crops to grow, when to plant them, and how to harvest them.

A poor harvest, however, could land tenant farmers in debt, owing back rent to the

Ella was her grandfather Ross's favorite grandchild. His nickname for her was "Grand Lady."

HORRID MASSACRE IN VIRGINIA.

The Scenes which the above Plate is designed to represent are—Fig. 1, a Mother intreating for the lives of her children.—2. Mr. Travis, cruelly murdered by his own Slaves.—3. Mr. Barrow, who bravely defended himself until his wife escaped.—4. A comp. of mounted Dragoons in pursuit of the Blacks.

Nineteenth-century woodcut depiction of the Southampton insurrection.
Credit: Library of Congress

During slavery, blacks were prohibited from learning to read and write. Slaves courageous enough to disobey the prohibitions against literacy risked being viciously beaten and even sold away from their families. Masters feared that a slave with the ability to read and write could more easily escape and even stir up rebellion among other slaves. After the Nat Turner Slave Rebellion on August 21, 1831, in Southampton County, Virginia, laws were enacted to make reading and writing punishable offenses.

Tenant Farmers

After the Civil War, most freed slaves found themselves with little education and few skills to earn a living. Thus, many remained on plantations as tenant farmers or sharecroppers, working land they rented from their former white masters.

Tenant farmers leased the equipment needed to plow the fields from the landlord or from the merchants who owned nearby stores. They also purchased the seed and fertilizer to grow the crops, along with the food to feed their families. From the spring planting to the fall harvest, whole families toiled in the fields. A share of the crops, such as cotton, tobacco, and rice, was used to pay the rent.

The unfair system of overpriced goods and services favored the landlords and entrapped black families in mounting debts. Black tenant farmers ended up tied to the land, much as they were during slavery.

African Americans picking cotton in Smithfield, N.C., 1940s–1950s.
Credit: Ellington Photo Collection, State Archives of North Carolina

plantation owner. More debt was incurred at the plantation store for the seed and supplies purchased, often at exorbitant markups. While the potential for independence existed, the financial means to break free generally eluded tenant farmers. Typically, they ended up dirt poor and chained to the land, just as during slavery.

Ella's parents heard stories about the harsh treatment the Bakers and Rosses suffered during slavery. This strengthened Blake's and Anna's resolve and determination to carve out a better life for themselves and for their children. Their ambitions were built on the foundation of their parents' difficult, but resilient, journey up from slavery. Blake and Anna extolled the virtues of hard, honest work while pushing their children to value education and excel in school.

School Days

During slavery, most slaves were denied any education and remained illiterate. Those who secretly defied the rules risked being severely punished. In spite of that, Ella's grandfather, Mitchell Ross, taught himself to read and write. In the next generation, his daughter Anna made an even bigger leap up the educational ladder. She was educated, trained as a teacher, and taught school in Littleton before getting married to Blake Baker.

By the time of emancipation, the southern economy was in ruins due to the Civil War. There was little money to spend on public school systems. Although more funds were gradually appropriated for education, the states intentionally underfunded African American schools, paid the teachers less, and provided fewer supplies than for white schools. A common practice was for states to transfer old, worn-out textbooks from the white schools to the black ones.

In rural farming communities, things were even worse. Often African American children walked several miles to and from the schools they attended, even when a white school was closer. The rundown black schoolhouses had battered furniture and, if lucky, might have a stove that provided heat in the winter. In contrast, white schools got two to three times as much state money, had better facilities, and had higher teachers' salaries.

Youngsters from rural, farming families did not have the luxury of attending school year-round. During the planting and harvesting seasons, children dropped out of school to pick crops such as cotton and tobacco. Despite the gross inequities in the separate education systems, African American families valued education and endured the associated hardships. They believed that educated persons would be better positioned to claim the full rights of citizenship as black freedoms were gradually won.

The Bakers made sure their children attended the best schools available and even paid for private schooling as they matured. In Littleton, Blake, Ella, and Maggie attended a free, two-room school attached to the South Street Baptist Church. Even before they went to school, Anna had taught them grammar, writing, and speech at home. When they enrolled in school, she kept in close touch with their teachers, knew them and the principals by name, and carefully monitored the children's homework.

Estey Hall, built in 1873, is the administrative center of the Shaw University campus. *Credit:* State Archives of North Carolina

In 1918, at fourteen, Ella, considered the smartest of the three children, was sent away to attend the high school division at Shaw Academy and University in Raleigh, North Carolina.[10] Founded in 1865, the university was originally named Raleigh Institute and started as a theological institution that trained African American males for the ministry. In 1866, the first class of women was admitted.

After completing her studies at Shaw Academy, Ella continued in the university division. She was a serious-minded scholar, but her years at the university

> **She [Ella] was a serious-minded scholar, but her years at the university were not without some tense moments of rebellion. She clashed with those in authority when she felt her rights, or those of the student body in general, had been abridged.**

were not without some tense moments of rebellion. She clashed with those in authority when she felt her rights, or those of the student body in general, had been abridged. Sometimes she was the spokesperson for groups of dissatisfied students, and at other times she spoke for herself.

The first protest came about when Ella was a senior in the high school division. She was asked to submit a petition, signed by women students, requesting that the school relax its dress code forbidding them to wear silk stockings on campus. As a student, Ella dressed modestly and did not concern herself with the latest in fashion, so she did not feel strongly about having the rule dropped. Nevertheless, she agreed to represent the students. They knew that she was an excellent speaker and skilled debater who would forcefully argue their case while not being intimidated by the administrators. Ella met several times with the dean of women, who was shocked by how tenaciously and assertively she argued the students' case. The dean denied the request, but by the time Baker graduated four years later, the rule had been removed from the dress code.

The next time Baker butted heads with a university official, she took a principled stand against the last white president of the institution. In explaining the incident, Baker put it in context:

> We raised questions about different kinds of things, and one thing in particular, I think, that irked him was that he would do the kind of thing that many students resented. When northern whites would come, they'd want you to sing spirituals. . . . I recall them asking me if I'd lead something. . . . But I said, "No, Mr. President."[11]

Ella Baker had disagreements with Charles Francis Meserve, the president of Shaw University, before graduating in 1927. *Credit:* J. A. Whitted, *A History of the Negro Baptists in North Carolina* (1908)

CHARLES FRANCIS MESERVE, LL.D., President Shaw University.

19th Amendment: Women's Voting Rights

The Nineteenth Amendment to the U.S. Constitution, ratified on August 18, 1920, gave women the right to vote. It stated: "The right of citizens of the United States to vote shall not be denied or abridged by the United States or by any State on account of sex."

The Voting Rights Act, ratified on August 6, 1965, aimed to overcome legal barriers at the state and local levels that prevented African Americans from exercising their right to vote under the Fifteenth and Nineteenth Amendments.

Newspaper article reporting the ratification of the Nineteenth Amendment.
Credit: Library of Congress

African American Suffragettes
Upper row (left to right): Nannie Helen Burroughs, Anna Julia Cooper, Elizabeth Piper Ensley, Frances Ellen Watkins Harper.
Bottom row (left to right): Daisy Elizabeth Adams Lampkin, Mary Church Terrell, Sojourner Truth, Ida B. Wells.
Credit: Library of Congress

What It Takes to Make a Change

The U.S. Congress has the power to change, or amend, the Constitution. The process begins when a two-thirds majority of the members of both the House of Representatives and the Senate agrees to the idea. Next the proposed amendment is sent to the governors of each state. The governors submit the amendment to their state legislatures for a vote. For the amendment to be added to the U.S. Constitution, three-fourths of the states must vote to approve it. Once that happens, the amendment is said to be ratified and becomes a law.

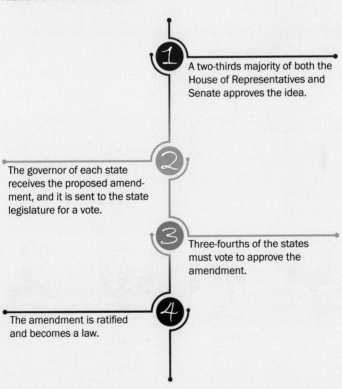

1. A two-thirds majority of both the House of Representatives and Senate approves the idea.

2. The governor of each state receives the proposed amendment, and it is sent to the state legislature for a vote.

3. Three-fourths of the states must vote to approve the amendment.

4. The amendment is ratified and becomes a law.

That was quite a bold stance for a student to take against the head of the institution.

During her junior year, Baker and a large group of other students refused to take the Bible examination required of all those enrolled. The students claimed that the exam was being administered unfairly by one professor in particular. When they received a negative response to their letter of protest, the majority of the students, including Ella, backed down and took the exam.

Despite these acts of rebellion against authority, overall Baker blossomed at the university and graduated in 1927 as valedictorian of her class. She left Shaw as a self-confident, well-read young woman eager to make her mark in the world.

Making Her Own Way

Next to Ella Baker's extended family, the black Baptist church was the most important influence in her life. From a young age, the church imprinted upon her a strong sense of morality, justice, and social obligation. Ella witnessed the Christian charity practiced by her mother and other churchwomen. From their examples, she learned to have empathy for others, whether they lived in her community or were perfect strangers.

Baker remembered how her mother nursed the sick and gladly aided total strangers. Anna fed, bathed, and washed the clothes of less fortunate children in their neighborhood. Often Ella was by her mother's side as she performed these acts of kindness. At other times, Anna assigned Ella chores of her own to do for needy families. Her mother's example instilled a like-minded sense of compassion in her daughter.

In the summer of 1927, at the age of twenty-three, Baker, the recent college graduate, left home for New

Jersey. She initially lived with a cousin while she got her bearings, found a job, and began earning some money. Having Ella in the embrace of family eased her mother's mind.

The first job she landed was as a waitress at a resort hotel. Her young coworkers were a disparate mix of aspiring show-business types comprised of blacks, whites, and even Europeans. She later credited them with teaching her a lot about life, especially how to read people. In the fall, Ella moved from New Jersey to New York City and settled in Harlem.

When Baker arrived in Harlem, it was bubbling with excitement. The Harlem Renaissance was in full bloom, and Harlem could rightly claim to be the center of African American artistic, cultural, and intellectual life in America. White audiences were receptive to experiencing black culture. People flocked to the vibrant community to listen to the music, hear poetry, attend plays, and experience art infused with racial pride. Well-established and aspiring authors and artists were prolific in their output and creativity.

Harlem opened up an eye-popping, stylishly urbane, and intellectually sophisticated world to Baker. She had to adjust to a noisy environment, with its nonstop street traffic and blaring sirens. On weekends, intoxicating jazz music poured out of the nightclubs and bars, jam packed with folks unwinding from the workweek. In 1934, a few years after Baker's arrival, the soon-to-be-famous Apollo

The Harlem Renaissance

Starting in the 1920s and lasting until the mid-1930s, a great cultural renaissance bloomed in New York City in Harlem, making it the cultural capital of black America. The rich lode of art emerging from this renaissance exposed the nation and, indeed, the world to artistic expressions that celebrated the uniqueness of black life.

The most prolific writer of the renaissance was Langston Hughes, a poet, novelist, playwright, and lyricist. In the vanguard with Hughes were highly praised writers such as Claude McKay, Jean Toomer, and Zora Neale Hurston.

Aspiring musicians experienced the genius and versatility of Duke Ellington, a pianist, conductor, and songwriter, and fans flocked to clubs to hear Bessie Smith, Billie Holiday, Jelly Roll Morton, and Louis Armstrong. Theater lovers might catch Paul Robeson on stage in his critically praised performances. Talent and race pride lit up Harlem.

The Apollo Theater in the 1940s. *Credit:* Library of Congress, William Gottlieb, photographer

Theater on 125th Street opened. The Monday evening auditions unearthed amateur performers who went on to become famous. Ella Fitzgerald and Pearl Bailey were two Amateur Night winners. Billie Holiday, Lena Horne, and the Count Basie Orchestra debuted there.

During the daytime, the busy blocks running from 115th Street uptown to 144th Street swarmed with people. The corner of Lenox Avenue (now Malcolm X Boulevard) and 135th Street was particularly busy. On hot summer evenings, Harlemites crowded the wide sidewalks of Lenox Avenue as they entered and exited the subway station or strolled along the avenue.

Passersby often stopped to listen as soapbox orators lectured on their political views, barked out various religious diatribes, and hawked medical potions that promised miracle cures for assorted illnesses. Popular speakers had loyal followers and on a good day attracted hundreds of listeners. Ella Baker heard speakers expressing revolutionary political views that captured her attention because they put into words the thoughts that had been stirring around in her head.

Ella Baker in the 1940s.
Credit: Library of Congress

Harlem on Her Mind

Ella's first priority once she got settled in Harlem was to find a job. Legions of young folks arrived in Harlem full of big dreams but low on money. Like them, she snatched whatever low-wage jobs came her way and worked a string of domestic and odd jobs.

Arriving two years before the Great Depression hit, Ella soon found herself in the midst of homelessness, long unemployment lines, and the devastating existence of people in poverty. The hungry men, women, and especially children cast a gloomy shadow over the giddy excitement of the Roaring Twenties. The daily suffering troubled Baker and sympathetic friends. They longed to relieve the human misery.

George Schuyler, a well-known black journalist and new acquaintance of Baker's, had an idea. Impatient to ease the poverty, Schuyler thought of creating a network of cooperative buying clubs that would purchase goods in bulk and sell them at reduced prices to members,

Breadline in the 1930s at McCauley Water Street Mission under the Brooklyn Bridge, New York. *Credit:* Library of Congress

The 1930s Depression

The Great Depression was a time when jobless, homeless, and hungry people lined up in breadlines and at soup kitchens for a free meal. Often the food handed out was their only meal of the day. The Depression took a heavy toll on African Americans. In Harlem, entire families were evicted from their homes. Others found shelter in damp basements and cramped cellars. It was a common site to see desperate, poverty-stricken women and children hunting through garbage cans for scraps of discarded food. With the onset of World War II, industrial and manufacturing companies began ramping up production and hiring workers to produce the weapons and other goods needed to fight the war. The nation's economy improved, which finally ended the Depression.

who would purchase shares in the clubs. In exchange for the discounted prices, the co-op members would run the business, stocking the shelves, ringing up sales, and doing whatever jobs had to be done.

Ella and her friends were keen on Schuyler's idea. Together they created the Young Negroes Cooperative League (YNCL) in 1930. Ella was appointed the first national director, with responsibility for organizing YNCL clubs

George Schuyler inspired Ella Baker and others to create the Young Negroes Cooperative League. *Credit:* Library of Congress, Carl Van Vechten, photographer

throughout the country. The financial viability of the cooperative depended on growing and sustaining club memberships. When the mass base of members did not materialize, YNCL folded after two years. Although the experiment in self-determination and economic self-sufficiency collapsed, Baker left her imprint on it.

She instituted democratic rules of operation for the clubs. Operationally, this meant eliminating any imbalance in the exercise of power that might occur between club members who had greater financial resources and those who had lesser. The rules for the cooperatives stated that each member had only one vote, no matter how many shares were purchased. So a person with one co-op share had the same influence and decision-making power as a person who owned multiple shares.

In meetings, it was understood that women's voices would carry as much weight as men's. Youth voices would also be heard and listened to. To ensure the participation of youth and young adults, the bylaws stated that two-thirds of a buying club's membership had to approve anyone over thirty-five who applied to join.[12] The YNCL turned out to be for Baker an important early training ground in community organizing.

The New York City Harlem branch library, the Young Men's Christian Association (YMCA), and the Young Women's Christian Association (YWCA) became favorite haunts for Baker. These were storied institutions that drew scores of those who were simply curious and others who were intensely serious. An eclectic mix of people came to socialize with old acquaintances, to make new friends, and to fiercely debate the roiling social, political, and economic issues of the day.

Spirited conversations about the stubbornly persistent, deeply rooted, and morally reprehensible injustices inflicted on blacks animated Baker, stimulating her political thinking and refining her increasingly radical views on social change. Could there be a better training ground for Baker, who yearned to fight for black civil rights?

In 1934, the Harlem branch library hired Baker to coordinate a youth and young adult education program. By then, she was thirty-one years old and welcomed the steady income. Within two years, Baker had initiated the Young People's Forum (YPF). Everything about YPF reflected Baker's style of empowering individuals to take responsibility for transforming their own lives and communities.

The first step was to embolden the youth and young adults by introducing them to the wider world beyond Harlem and getting them excited about previously unimagined possibilities. Baker stimulated their minds through books, daring them to think boldly and creatively. Exposure to accomplished artists and professionals raised their aspirations. Baker also connected YPF with other youth programs in Harlem and throughout the city. Her guiding hand overhauled an initial program idea into a robust, much-expanded, and comprehensive project. YPF was an early example of what became a familiar pattern in Baker's efforts to transform communities by transforming people.

> Everything about YPF reflected Baker's style of empowering individuals to take responsibility for transforming their own lives and communities.

Dorothy Height, president of the National Council of Negro Women, was a friend of Baker's. *Credit:* Library of Congress

The YWCA had influenced Baker's life since her youth. As a college student, she joined the campus YWCA chapter. Her first visit to New York City, with a Shaw student delegation to a YWCA meeting, made a lasting impression on her.

Baker spent many hours in the Harlem YWCA cafeteria and meeting rooms. She was especially drawn to the strong-minded, intelligent young women who gathered there and formed lifelong friendships. One such friendship was with Dorothy I. Height, who later became the president of the National Council of Negro Women, a position she held for over forty years. Another close YWCA pal was Pauli Murray, a fellow North Carolinian who became a distinguished civil rights lawyer, religious leader, and feminist poet.

In the 1960s, decades after her work at the Harlem YWCA, Baker worked at the Atlanta branch, traveling throughout the South conducting race relations workshops. Baker always found a welcoming home at the YWCA, an affiliation that wove a bright thread of enrichment throughout her life from adolescence to adulthood.

Pauli Murray *(above)* and Ella Baker met at the Harlem YWCA and remained lifelong friends.
Credit: Library of Congress

The NAACP Years

In 1940, Ella Baker became an assistant field secretary at the national office of the NAACP in New York City. Since its founding in 1909, the NAACP had become the premier civil rights organization in America, so Baker was happy to land the job. She was also relieved to have the steady income.

Baker's assignment was to build the membership rolls of the NAACP branches scattered throughout the South. The hours were long, the schedules grueling, and the speaking engagements endless and exhausting. She went where assigned, sometimes to cities, including her first trip to Birmingham, Alabama, to launch a major membership drive. Other days, she found herself in out-of-the-way rural communities such as Farmville, Virginia. Self-assured and gutsy, Baker seldom worried about her personal safety when traveling alone, or the comfort of the accommodations that awaited her.

W. E. B. DuBois *(front row, fifth from the left)* and other members of the NAACP in 1929. *Credit:* Library of Congress

In the field, Baker, unassuming in her manner, dressed like the folks who attended her meetings and spoke in plain, everyday language. She recruited in poolrooms, bars, barbershops, nightclubs, and other unconventional venues where ordinary folk congregated. Her mingling with common people in everyday places outraged and shocked some of her colleagues, who preferred appealing to middle-class audiences in more conventional settings such as churches. Baker was accused of exhibiting unladylike behavior and flaunting the expected code of conduct.

Staying focused on the purpose of her visits and what she hoped to accomplish, Baker pressed on. The greatly expanded membership rolls attested to her effectiveness, as did some of her colleagues. The Washington, D.C., branch president, Herbert Marshall, commended Baker's skills and insights as an organizer.[13] E. Frederic Morrow, a peer and fellow field secretary, doffed his hat, concluding that Baker's "success in the past few months with the Association has been phenomenal."[14]

Within three years, the NAACP promoted Baker to national director of branches, a post she held from 1943 to 1946. During her tenure, the memberships swelled ninefold, and the organization extended its presence into untapped territories. Baker brought a participatory, group-centered approach to branch operations. This minimized hierarchy so that leaders and projects bubbled up from the bottom. With consensus decision making, the strategies and plans that emerged would be owned by the local groups responsible for implementing them.

In an instance of initial opposition to her presence, Baker's unflagging energy and ability to connect with ordinary people won over a skeptical John M. Tinsley, the Richmond, Virginia, branch president and state chairman. Tinsley had requested that national staff help with the annual statewide membership campaign. Walter White, the NAACP's executive secretary and top official, notified him that Baker would be coming. Tinsley wrote back requesting a "young Man" as more suitable for the assignment because the personal accommodations might not be comfortable in every locality.[15] By the time White received the request, Baker was already on her way to Virginia.

However, by the campaign's end, Tinsley wrote praising Baker's hard work and boasting about how she had gained the trust and cooperation of community leaders. Speaking at an NAACP conference in 1942, Baker explained that "persons living and working in a community are in a better position to select leadership for a community project than one coming into the community."[16]

Training grassroots leaders to help them do their jobs better was always a high priority for Baker. She initiated a series of regional leadership training conferences. The purpose was to give staff and volunteers the opportunity to acquire the basic skills needed to plan and execute programs and, importantly, to sustain them. Pauli Murray, whom Baker first met at the Harlem YWCA in the 1920s and with whom she remained friends, wrote high-level NAACP officials to support Baker's proposed training program.

Finally given the nod to go ahead, Baker convened well-attended leadership conferences in Shreveport, Louisiana; Tulsa, Oklahoma; Atlanta, Georgia; Jacksonville, Florida; Chicago, Illinois; Easton, Pennsylvania; and Indianapolis, Indiana. Roy Wilkins, an NAACP official and frequent adversary and critic of Baker, praised the conferences as among her main contributions to the organization.

"A common word used to describe her was 'difficult.'" She owned this assessment of herself, if *difficult* meant that "she did not ingratiate herself with those in high positions, and she did not hesitate to speak her mind even when her ideas were controversial."

In 1946, after six years, Baker resigned her NAACP post and was characteristically honest in explaining why: "I feel that the Association is falling short of its present possibilities; that the full capacities of the staff have not been used; that there is little chance of mine being utilized in the immediate future."[17]

Baker never hesitated to criticize when frustrated and disappointed. In those moments, she could be a severe and unrelenting critic, one who aimed piercing, accusatory words at the offending parties. In addition to Walter White and Roy Wilkins, who suffered the slings and arrows of Baker's words, some colleagues "found Baker's manner abrasive and her straightforward style annoying. A common word used to describe her was 'difficult.'"[18] She owned this assessment of herself, if *difficult* meant that "she did not ingratiate herself with those in high positions, and she did not hesitate to speak her mind even when her ideas were controversial."[19]

After leaving the NAACP, Baker held short-term jobs with civil rights and community service organizations over the next six years. In 1952, the New York City NAACP appointed her the branch president, the first woman to hold the position. Having been active in the branch for several years, Baker was familiar with the political landscape and current issues in the city. She made a significant symbolic change by moving the branch headquarters from downtown New York City to Harlem, the heart of the black community. She also reached out to engage branch members in NAACP programs.

Baker campaigned for issues that affected blacks, such as integrated schools to deliver a quality public education for all New York City students, and for police accountability and fair treatment of people of color. She intentionally sought out organizations that had complementary agendas in order to build coalitions. To her credit, she was able to navigate tactfully and skillfully around the personality conflicts and jealous rivalries that often stalled groups seeking to come together. Even with a full agenda of progressive issues to champion at the Harlem branch, by the late 1950s Baker longed to get back into the fray on the southern front of the civil rights movement, where momentous victories had stirred people to mass action.

SCLC Keeps the Protest Spirit Alive

Poor-quality schools and restrictions on voting had assigned southern blacks to second-class citizenship since the days of slavery. In the 1950s, however, successive judicial and legislative triumphs heralded a new day and pried the door open for blacks to demand more.

On May 17, 1954, the U.S. Supreme Court handed down a unanimous decision in the case *Brown v. Board of Education of Topeka*, mandating that separate schools for black and white students were unconstitutional. Three years later, the U.S. Congress passed the Civil Rights Act of 1957, aimed at ensuring voting rights for African Americans. These were hopeful signs of a changing racial climate, though hardened resistance would delay and thwart full compliance for decades to come.

In the midst of the social upheaval, blacks in Montgomery, Alabama, turned an unexpected act of

Photo of Rosa Parks taken at her booking after she was arrested for refusing to give up her seat to a white passenger on a bus in Montgomery, Ala., on December 1, 1955. *Photo in the public domain*

civil disobedience on a city bus into a protest movement. It happened on December 1, 1955, when Rosa Parks, a seamstress employed by the Montgomery Fair department store and secretary to the local NAACP branch, refused to give up her seat on the Cleveland Avenue bus to a white man.

Blacks constituted the majority of bus riders in Montgomery. In particular, black women used the buses to ride to jobs as domestic workers in white homes. "Jim Crow" segregation laws required black passengers to sit in the back of the bus. Historically, black women were subjected to rude and discourteous treatment and sometimes physical and sexual abuse by white bus drivers and even by policemen.

Brown v. Board of Education

In 1950, the Brown family lived in an integrated neighborhood In Topeka, Kansas. However, Linda, the daughter of Leola and Oliver Brown, was forced to travel a significant distance to attend an all-black elementary school, although the all-white Sumner Elementary School was closer to her home. The state had a dual system of public schools that were supposed to be separate but equal.

At the urging of the NAACP, Oliver Brown attempted to enroll Linda in the third grade at Sumner, but she was denied admission. The NAACP combined the Browns' complaint with similar cases from different states and filed a legal suit against the Topeka school board. The case became known as *Brown v. Board of Education of Topeka, Kansas*.

After an unfavorable decision from the U.S. district court in Kansas, the U.S. Supreme Court agreed to hear the case. Thurgood Marshall, the chief counsel for the NAACP Legal Defense and Educational Fund, argued the case, asking the court to dismantle the South's entire system of segregated schools.

On May 17, 1954, Chief Justice Earl Warren read the unanimous decision. In part, it said: "We conclude that, in the field of public education, the doctrine of 'separate but equal' has no place. Separate educational facilities are inherently unequal."

Nettie Hunt and her daughter Nickie sit on the steps of the U.S. Supreme Court. Nettie explains to her daughter the meaning of the high court's ruling in the *Brown v. Board of Education* case about segregation in public schools is unconstitutional, 1954. *Credit:* Library of Congress Prints and Photographs Division, Washington, D.C.

As the *Brown* decision struck down segregation in public education, southern states threw up obstacles to prevent the law from being enforced. An extreme example was Prince Edward County, Virginia, which shut down its entire public education system in protest. The schools remained closed until 1964, when the Supreme Court ruled against the county.

It was North Carolina native Edward R. Murrow, a well-known and highly respected radio and TV news broadcaster, who brought the story of Prince Edward County to the public's attention when he aired a national documentary on the CBS television network titled "The Lost Class of '59."

Rosa Parks was not just a tired, soft-spoken middle-aged lady who refused to give up her seat that evening. She was "a militant race woman, a sharp detective, and an anti-rape activist."[20] In 1944, the NAACP branch office in Montgomery sent Parks to Abbeville, Alabama, to investigate the kidnapping and brutal gang rape of Recy Taylor, a twenty-four-year-old wife, mother, and sharecropper. In the Taylor case, the raised voices of African American women provoked local, national, and even international outrage and extended the campaigns for racial justice and human dignity.

Black women like Parks flew swiftly to the defense of their black sisters when they suffered rape and sexualized violence at the hands of white men and faced a hostile and indifferent judicial system. In fact, it was the Women's Political Council of the Montgomery NAACP that sprang into action as soon as Mrs. Parks was arrested for refusing to give up her bus seat. The ensuing chain of events resulted in a 381-day bus boycott that ended with the court-ordered desegregation of the buses.

The entire civil rights community, in and outside the South, rallied to support the Montgomery movement. Ella Baker was among them. She praised it as an event that was "unpredicted, where thousands of individuals, just black ordinary people, subjected themselves to inconveniences that were certainly beyond the thinking of most folk."[21] Baker, and other sympathetic friends in New York, wondered what could be done to sustain the mass action.

The Montgomery Improvement Association was established to oversee the boycott, and its leaders, including Dr. Martin Luther King Jr., were pondering the same questions. King approached two of his most trusted advisors—Bayard Rustin, a brilliant civil rights strategist, and Stanley David Levison, a white, Jewish attorney— to draw up preliminary plans for a

Bayard Rustin convinced Dr. Martin Luther King Jr. to hire Ella Baker. *Credit:* Library of Congress

permanent organization that would coordinate other mass-action protests.

Rustin and Levison knew they needed a person skilled in community organizing to assist them. Ella Baker came immediately to mind. She was a well-respected and highly capable community organizer with a network of contacts throughout the South. At first, King was not keen on the idea of having a woman on the team, one who would eventually share the leadership role with him. Rustin and Levison insisted and finally

SCLC button.
Credit: Shaw University

convinced King that Baker was the person needed. When asked, she agreed and joined the team. Within a year, on January 10, 1957, the Southern Christian Leadership Conference (SCLC) was founded. The word *Christian* was included in the organization's name to reflect its grounding in the fundamentals of the Christian faith and to deflect any accusations of influence by nonreligious and nondemocratic political ideologies, such as communism. In the Cold War era, the idea that communism would subvert democracy was feared. Civil rights organizations were especially vulnerable to such suspicions.

Eventually, Baker was hired by SCLC as the first associate director and later as the interim director. King relied on her heavily, although he never warmed toward her. Baker was not the only woman excluded from King's inner circle. None of the women on the front lines during the Montgomery bus boycott were invited to serve in leadership positions. Baker recognized that sexism influenced King's attitude. Further, there was a deep strain of elitism that Baker bluntly called out, saying, "After all, who was I? I was female, I was old. I didn't have any Ph.D."[22] Baker took the arm's-length relationship in stride because she would be helping to create a new organization that had tremendous potential to advance the movement.

In 1957, Baker agreed to coordinate the logistics of the first major SCLC event, the Prayer Pilgrimage for Freedom, held at the Lincoln Memorial on May 17, on the third anniversary of the *Brown v. Board* decision. The expected outcome was unclear, but the large turnout, estimated at between 25,000 and 30,000, and King's moving speech got him an invitation to meet with Vice President Richard M. Nixon. In the meeting a month later, King called for the administration to use its voice to urge southerners to comply with the *Brown v. Board* school desegregation ruling and to support black voting rights. In August, Congress passed the hotly debated 1957 Civil Rights Act, which had been in the works for a few months. It was primarily a voting rights bill.

Early on, SCLC had decided that voting rights would be a priority, with the goal of massively increasing the number of registered black voters. States in the Deep South, and the border states, routinely disqualified African Americans through the use of literacy tests, poll taxes, and arbitrary restrictions.

A year after the Prayer Pilgrimage, SCLC launched an ambitious regional voter registration campaign, called the Crusade for Citizenship. At an October meeting, King announced that the kickoff would begin by February in at least ten cities simultaneously. There would be mass meetings to appeal to blacks to register and registration classes to support those making the attempt. However, no administrative infrastructure was in place to support the crusade.

February 12, 1958, was the launch date for the kickoff, chosen to commemorate the birthday of Abraham Lincoln, who issued the Emancipation Proclamation. Levison and Rustin persuaded a reluctant King to bring in Baker to coordinate the event. This time she was hired and became the first full-time SCLC staff member. Using her network of contacts, many of them at the NAACP (although that organization had not officially endorsed the crusade), Baker quickly arranged kickoff events in twenty-one cities. Church rallies, press conferences, and prayer vigils were held.

Despite her tireless efforts, which King recognized, the kickoff fell short of expectations, as did subsequent attempts over the next few

An oral history interviewer concluded that "Although the SCLC needed Baker's skills, it was not willing to recognize or affirm her leadership." The other leaders seemed to respect her abilities but feared her independence.

months to register masses of new voters. After eighteen months, King was forced to admit that, as historian Taylor Branch has written, "the Crusade for Citizenship had failed. Fund-raising and registration totals fell dismally short of the goals announced at the outset."[23]

From the beginning, the SCLC relationship was challenging for Baker. There were drastic, fundamental, and nonnegotiable differences between Baker's philosophy of organizing mass movements for radical social transformation and the SCLC's way of operating. Baker emphasized putting processes in place that would sustain direct-action campaigns, rather than single dramatic, leader-centered events like the Prayer Pilgrimage. Engaging more women and youth in planning programs was a priority for her.

Then, there were the ever-present frustrations, similar to those at the NAACP, with the undisguised sexism. The search for a SCLC director was a particularly stinging example. While Baker had run the SCLC office efficiently and performed the duties of a director since the organization's inception, she was overlooked in two searches for a permanent replacement. An oral history interviewer concluded that "Although the SCLC needed Baker's skills, it was not willing to recognize or affirm her leadership."[24] The other leaders seemed to respect her abilities but feared her independence. By 1960, Baker was ready to move on.

The Birth of SNCC

I n the decades after the Civil War, social customs and, later, Jim Crow laws mandated strict separation of the races. Communities throughout the South maintained separate public facilities. There were separate black schools, separate black libraries, separate YMCA and YWCA branches, separate parks and swimming pools. Blacks were prohibited from drinking at the same water fountains or using the same restrooms as whites. At train and interstate bus stations, there were segregated black waiting rooms with separate entrances. At movie theaters, blacks were restricted to seating in the balcony, nicknamed the crows' nest. Even more belittling, some high-end department stores did not allow black customers to try on clothes; others had separate entrances for blacks and whites. The African American facilities were nearly always inferior and second rate.

Protesters pray before a sit-in at the Royal Ice Cream Parlor in Durham, N.C. *Credit:* Durham County Public Library

This southern brand of racial separatism angered black college students, especially those from the North and Midwest, who were encountering the rigid color line for the first time. As early as the 1940s, students staged protests in several cities.

In 1943 and 1944, Howard University students sat in at public places in Washington, D.C., hoping to spark protests across the nation. However, university president Mordecai Johnson ended the sit-ins. Black college presidents were often pressured by white donors, civic leaders, and state higher education authorities to halt such protests. Retaliation in the form of reduced, or withheld, financial support hung over their heads.

A few years later, in 1957, six young protesters, led by a local minister, sat in at Durham's Royal Ice Cream Parlor. The next year, the NAACP Youth Council in Wichita, Kansas, organized a sit-in at Dockum's Drug Store, which was later recognized as the first successful sit-in of the civil rights movement. In that same year, the Katz drugstore in Oklahoma City integrated in response to an NAACP Youth Council sit-in.

A rising tide of social change also coincided with the student sit-ins in the 1940s and 1950s. Having fought for American democracy on the battlefields of Europe during World War II, black soldiers returned to the United States with their eyes wide open to the stark differences between the liberties and freedoms they had experienced abroad and the rigidly enforced racial segregation at home. In addition, freedom's door was opened wider when executive orders issued by President Franklin D. Roosevelt in 1941 and President Harry Truman in 1948 banned discriminatory employment practices in the defense industry and segregation in the armed services.

Race issues continued to weigh heavily on the minds of black college students, who were still chafing under the heavy yoke of discrimination. Located in a close-knit black community on the east side of Greensboro, North Carolina Agricultural and Technical College (later known as A&T University) and Bennett College were neighboring institutions, one private, the

On the second day of the Greensboro sit-in, Joseph A. McNeil and Franklin E. McCain were joined by William Smith and Clarence Henderson at the Woolworth lunch counter. *Credit: Greensboro News and Record*

other public. In 1959, Bennett students talked about protesting at downtown businesses. John Hatchett, the faculty advisor to the campus NAACP chapter, recalled that "from September until early November we met constantly and discussed viable strategies to implement our [protest] goals."[25] Students at North Carolina A&T held similar discussions.

At one point, activists on both campuses held joint meetings to plot strategies for a protest. However, on February 1, 1960, Ezell A. Blair Jr. (later Jibreel Khazan),

Franklin E. McCain, Joseph A. McNeil, and David L. Richmond, four A&T freshmen, decided impulsively to act without consulting their peers. Perhaps the final straw was McNeil's experience at the local Greyhound bus terminal. On his return to campus after the winter holidays, he had been denied counter service. On the fateful late afternoon of the sit-in, the neatly dressed young men left Scott Hall and walked the short distance to downtown. They entered the Woolworth store at the corner of South Elm and Sycamore Streets (now February One Place), purchased some school supplies, then sat down at the whites-only lunch counter and politely ordered coffee. They were refused service but peacefully stayed there until the store was closed and then returned to campus.

The very act of sitting at the lunch counter violated long-established Woolworth policy and accepted social customs. In an interview, one student explained that "We believe, since we buy books and papers in the other part of the store, we should get served in this part."[26]

The next day, students from other colleges joined the protest. Before long, black students from A&T, Bennett, and Dudley High School came to occupy the lunch counter stools. Soon white students from Woman's College and Guilford College, as well as adults, joined them. Protesters returned to the lunch counter day in and day out for several months. The police began arresting the demonstrators until busloads filled the jails to overflowing.

Greensboro Four statue on the campus of North Carolina A&T State University. *Credit:* Howard Gaither Photography

By late July, Mayor George H. Roach and Ed Zane, chairman of the newly formed Greensboro Advisory Committee on Community Relations, had persuaded the Woolworth management to negotiate a settlement. On Monday, July 25, 1960, the lunch counter was finally opened to "serve all properly dressed and well-behaved people."[27] In a gesture of respect, the manager, Clarence Harris, invited the store's four African American employees—Charles Bess, Mattie Long, Susie Morrison, and Jamie Robinson—to be the first to eat at the counter. The sit-ins initiated by the "Greensboro Four," as the A&T students became known, sparked a movement that spread like wildfire to fifty-five other cities and thirteen states.[28]

While student leaders were gratified by the relatively quick victories, the NAACP and SCLC leaders were vexed. They viewed the sit-ins as an incursion into their own well-staked-out territory of black advocacy. Notwithstanding these objections, the NAACP and SCLC officials were eager to find out more about the student movement. Baker contacted the student leaders on behalf of SCLC and opened a dialogue with them.

Initially, King lobbied to incorporate the sit-in movement into SCLC. The NAACP also made an overture, but the students chose to remain autonomous. Baker agreed with them. She summed up the resulting friction this way: "I think the basic reason for the reactions of the NAACP and SCLC to the students is the fact that they elected to be independent and they exercised the independence [in ways] that only young people . . . can. They were open to ideas that would not have been . . . tolerated by either the NAACP or SCLC."[29]

Roy Wilkins, the NAACP executive director, was extremely harsh in his criticism, saying that "They don't take orders from anybody; they don't consult anybody. They operate in a kind of vacuum." "When the headlines are gone," he continued, "the issues still have to be settled in court."[30] The students, however, refused to be browbeaten by the NAACP and SCLC leaders. They would chart their own course.

From the outset, it was apparent to Baker that the students lacked the organizing skills, leadership

Those who formed SNCC met on the Shaw campus (*at left*), and Martin Luther King Jr. spoke at Memorial Auditorium (*at right*). *Credit:* Albert Barden Collection, State Archives of North Carolina

experience, or political sophistication to sustain the movement they spawned. Baker also knew that her expertise could help them and offered it at a conference convened in Raleigh in the spring. An eight-hundred-dollar grant from the SCLC covered the cost.

The conference convened on Easter weekend (April 15–17, 1960) at Shaw University, Baker's alma mater. She "was hoping for not more than, say, a hundred and some of the 'leadership' of the sit-ins as we had culled it from the newspapers and so forth. . . . It ended up [with] about three hundred or more people."[31] Delegates representing fifty-eight sit-in centers and additional delegates from nineteen northern colleges attended. The fact that Martin Luther King Jr. had jointly signed the letter of invitation and would be speaking was an enormous draw.

Martin Luther King Jr. at a meeting in Raleigh, April 16, 1960.
Credit: News and Observer Collection, State Archives of North Carolina

As described in the letter of invitation, students would have the opportunity "TO SHARE experience gained in recent protest demonstrations and TO HELP chart future goals for effective action."[32] Students exchanged ideas, renewed friendships, and explored the possibilities for future actions. By the end, a decision had been made to found their own organization, the Student Nonviolent Coordinating Committee (SNCC). Baker knew that it was important for the students to meet adults on an equal footing and not be manipulated or dominated by them, as the SNCC leaders anticipated would happen if they were under the umbrella of an established organization.

In an article entitled "Bigger than a Hamburger," Baker applauded the idealism of the students and made the case that their protest was about more than a hamburger and a Coke.[33] The protesters sought ambitiously "to rid America of the scourge of racial segregation and discrimination." She confessed that many schools and communities had "not provided adequate experience for young Negroes to assume initiative and think and act independently [which] accentuated the need for guarding the student movement against well-meaning, but nevertheless unhealthy, over-protectiveness." Baker hoped, ideally, that both the adults who engaged with the students and the young activists themselves would, in the end, develop each "individual to his highest potential for the benefit of the group."

SNCC was without financial resources, so Baker provided office space at the Atlanta headquarters of SCLC. The first official meeting convened there on May 13–14, 1960, with a group of eleven students in attendance. Baker also recruited Jane Stembridge, the daughter of a white Baptist minister and student at Union Theological Seminary in New York City, to run the office. Stembridge, who interrupted her seminary studies to become the first SNCC staff member, wrote a friend saying, "I came here because I, too, needed to be free, respected, understood. . . . Being white doesn't answer your problems, being able to go in anywhere does not end your needs."[34]

James Lawson, a divinity school student at Vanderbilt University who served as the southern director of the

Congress of Racial Equality (CORE), drafted a statement of purpose positioning SNCC as a nonviolent protest movement. The statement declared:

> We affirm the philosophical or religious ideal of nonviolence as the foundation of our purpose, the pre-supposition of our faith, and the manner of our action. Nonviolence as it grows from Judaic-Christian traditions seeks a social order of justice permeated by love. Integration of human endeavor represents the crucial first step towards such a society.[35]

The commitment to nonviolent principles, however, would diminish as the black power advocates assumed leadership of SNCC in the mid-1960s.

Historical marker commemorating the founding of SNCC on the campus of Shaw University. *Credit:* N.C. Office of Archives and History

Mentoring the Sit-In Students

Ella Baker had long held and acted on the belief "that the most effective leaders are . . . more interested in developing leadership in others than in getting recognition for their individual achievements."[36] SNCC offered Baker an opportunity to mold the next generation of young civil rights leaders. Attending her first SNCC meeting in 1964, Jean Wiley, an English instructor at Tuskegee Institute, observed Baker's hands-on, personal touch and said that "Ella Baker gathered and mentored us."[37] The SNCC students were the sprouting vines of the next generation of civil rights leaders and living testimonials to Baker's nurturing influence. Many of her protégés devoted their lives to politics and humanitarian causes.

A founding member and the third national chairman of SNCC (1963–1966), John Lewis was an exceptionally

John Lewis. *Credit:* Library of Congress

loyal Baker acolyte. He helped organize sit-ins at segregated lunch counters and participated in the Freedom Rides in 1961. Lewis has spent a lifetime in public service, including serving Georgia's Fifth Congressional District in the U.S. House of Representatives beginning in 1986. In explaining how Baker gained acceptance despite being of another generation, he said, "She was much older in terms of age, but I think in terms of ideas and philosophy and commitment she was one of the youngest persons in the movement."[38]

Julian Bond, another founding member, left Morehouse College in his final semester to become the SNCC director of communications. He later served four terms in the Georgia house and six in the Georgia senate. He served eleven years as national president of the NAACP.

An exemplary student activist, Marion Barry served

as SNCC's first national chairman and launched a chapter in Washington, D.C. Barry's public service began with a seat on the District of Columbia school board, followed by election to the city council. After three years on the council, he won the first of four terms as mayor.

Julian Bond. *Credit:* Library of Congress

Baker also inspired young women. She was a nontraditional role model much different from other women the students typically would have known at church back home, or among the female faculty at their colleges, or in the membership ranks of sororities and women's social service organizations.

Joanne Grant's friendship with Baker began when they connected at a SNCC meeting. Grant remembered Baker's rescuing her as she watched a heated dispute escalate into a scuffle and dissolved into tears. "Miss Baker, who was sitting next to me, stood up, pulled me to my feet and began to sing 'We Shall Overcome,' the song she called 'old soothing syrup.' It worked. She cooled it down."[39] Grant, a reporter, wrote a book about Baker entitled *Ella Baker: Freedom Bound* and produced the award-winning film *Fundi: The Story of Ella Baker*, documenting the instrumental role Baker played in the movement.[40] Baker was affectionately known as "the Fundi," which in Swahili means "a person who passes skills from one generation to the next."

While a student at Fisk University in Nashville, Tennessee, Diane Nash, a native of Chicago, experienced the humiliations of southern racism for the first time. Shocked by what she witnessed, Nash sought out civil disobedience training and participated in workshops conducted by James Lawson. She led the Freedom Rides in Nashville, was a founding member of SNCC, and became one of the few women who rose to national prominence in SNCC.

Soon after graduating from Yale Law School, Eleanor Holmes (Norton) met Baker and became a SNCC volunteer. She praised Baker as a doer and not just a talker. Later in her career, she became the first woman to chair the U.S. Equal Employment Opportunity Commission. Since 1991 Norton has served as the District of Columbia delegate to the U.S. House of Representatives.

There were many gifted and capable women in SNCC. However, the male leadership mirrored the sexism and male-dominated hierarchy that characterized the treatment of women, including Baker, in the NAACP and in the SCLC. Women who managed, despite the sexism, to ascend to leadership roles had to fight for inclusion, visibility, and a voice in decision making.

SNCC promotional literature depicted the interracial nature of the group.
Credit: Shaw University

A New Mission for a New Day

After the first wave of lunch counter sit-ins, there was a lull in youth-led mass-action protests. SNCC leaders had to figure out what came next. Two possibilities were debated.

The first was to have SNCC engage in on-the-ground, direct-action campaigns, similar to the original sit-ins. Taking direct action meant plowing familiar ground that students understood well, at a functional level, which they had done successfully. In addition, being on the front lines in transforming the offensive racial customs of southern society would have appealed to students, who were impatient for change.

Another strategy they considered was to launch a voter registration campaign, aimed at massively increasing the number of black voters in the South. Development of a political agenda was an uncharted course, one that was strongly urged upon SNCC by Robert F. Kennedy, the U.S. attorney general. Securing black voters to support President John F. Kennedy's bid for reelection in 1964 was a White House priority.

The mainstream civil rights organizations had also stressed the urgency of registering black voters. Through the ballot, blacks could elect officeholders who supported social change and were committed to protecting black rights. This would, and did, eventually transform the political landscape of the South.

Students who favored direct-action campaigns were adamantly opposed to the voter registration strategy, so much so that they were willing to leave SNCC if they lost. At the next SNCC meeting, held at the Highlander Folk School, Ella Baker proposed a compromise solution to the impasse. She recalled that "this was about the only time I made any special effort to influence."[41]

Baker suggested setting up two wings of operation within SNCC and dividing the staff between them. One wing would concentrate on direct-action projects and the other on voter registration campaigns. Students agreed to this pragmatic solution.

Rather than choosing one strategy to the exclusion of the other, Baker suggested setting up two wings of operation within SNCC and dividing the staff between them. One wing would concentrate on direct-action projects and the other on voter registration campaigns. Students agreed to this pragmatic solution. The compromise spared the nascent organization from splitting up and avoided the danger of "nobody accomplishing anything." With the capable assistance of James Forman, the new executive director of SNCC, the compromise was executed.

The first test of the dual strategy came late in the summer of 1961, when SNCC conducted workshops on nonviolent tactics in Mississippi and started voter registration drives there in the town of McComb and nearby rural counties. Violent confrontations between the voter registration volunteers and Mississippi authorities resulted in staff arrests, beatings, and the murder of two local residents. Bob Moses, the SNCC staff member who headed the project, was arrested and convicted on the charge of interfering with the police in the discharge of their duties. Bob Zellner, the white SNCC field secretary, had his eye gouged by white attackers.

Such extreme violence was the norm in Mississippi. Freedom fighters, and the local people who aided them, lived in fear. Joanne Grant recalled how she came to appreciate the danger students courted in Mississippi and the high esteem in which other students held them.

In 1961, she was assigned to cover a SNCC conference in Atlanta for the *National Guardian*, a weekly newspaper. "When the delegation from Mississippi entered the conference hall, the entire assembly stood in tribute to those who were struggling in the toughest state."[42]

But Mississippi was not the only state where dangers lurked. At the same conference, Grant watched as a group of Atlanta volunteers, preparing to sit in at the Magnolia Room restaurant at Rich's Department Store, sang an old gospel hymn as they were departing.

> "This may be the last time. This may be the last time, brother. This may be the last time. It may be the last time, I don't know." The recognition of what they were facing sobered me: this might be the last time that they would be together, the last day of their lives.[43]

After the brutal violence of Mississippi and the deliberate failure of Mississippi law enforcement, the state judicial system, and the Federal Bureau of Investigation to protect SNCC workers, students had to reassess the efficacy of nonviolent strategies as the best means for bringing about revolutionary change in the established social order. White violence opened the door for the raised voices of black power advocates to come in and promote more militant tactics of direct-action resistance.

Ella's Protégés

In a testimonial to Baker's influence in their lives and later career choices, several of the SNCC student leaders became national leaders.

Julian Bond served in the both the Georgia state house and senate. He served as head of the Southern Poverty Law Center and was president of the National Association for the Advancement of Colored People (NAACP).

Stokely Carmichael was national chair of SNCC (1966) but lost faith in nonviolence. He joined the Black Panther Party (1969) and advocated for black power, saying, "If we are to proceed toward true liberation, we must cut ourselves off from white people."

Eleanor Holmes Norton graduated from Yale Law School and worked alongside Fannie Lou Hamer on black voter registration in Mississippi. Since 1991 Norton has served as the District of Columbia delegate to the U.S. House of Representatives.

John Lewis has represented the Fifth Congressional District of Georgia in the U.S. House of Representatives since 1987. On March 7, 1965, while serving as SNCC chair (1963–1966), Lewis was viciously beaten during what came to be called Bloody Sunday.

Bob Moses had a passion for teaching and was awarded a prestigious MacArthur Fellowship "Genius Grant" in 1982. He used the prize money to create the Algebra Project, which pioneered a widely successful method of teaching algebra skills to minority students.

Diane Nash challenged segregation in Nashville, Tennessee, while an undergraduate at Fisk University. She played an important role in the Freedom Rides, the famous 1963 March on Washington, and the Selma, Alabama, voting rights campaign.

Photo credits: Library of Congress

The Black Power Struggle within SNCC

Although black college students started the lunch counter sit-ins, socially progressive white students soon protested alongside them, suffering the same verbal abuses and physical attacks. The racially diverse group of activists coalesced around the mutually shared goal of winning black civil rights. Demonstrating the same hard work and dedicated service as their black compatriots meant that whites eventually ascended to key leadership positions in SNCC.

In 1966, when Stokely Carmichael, a black power advocate, unseated John Lewis as the chairman, the debate over control of SNCC boiled over.[44] Those identifying strongly with the black power, black separatist ideology were concerned about maintaining black control of SNCC, a fear that was not exclusive to SNCC.

Other civil rights groups grappled with the issue of white participation and white financial support. They were fearful that it might lead to undue influence over the directions, means, and methods of black protest.

Stokely Carmichael replaced John Lewis as SNCC chairman in 1966. *Credit:* Library of Congress

After heated debate within SNCC, it was initially agreed that students would be assigned to communities that corresponded to their race. White activists would organize in white communities, while the black activists would continue in black communities. Later, however, SNCC leaders voted to expel the white staff, then quickly changed their minds and decided that whites could stay, but without voting rights. Only seven white staff members stayed on.[45]

The black power ideal was to instill a sense of racial pride in African Americans. Its message of self-help and self-determination sought to overcome the scars of racism, physical brutality, and sexual exploitation inflicted during slavery, and the humiliating racial segregation and discrimination experienced after emancipation. The writings and speeches of Malcolm X fueled the movement, arguing for a change in mind-set. Rather than seeing themselves as powerless victims, blacks were pressed to seize the initiative in bringing about social, political, and economic change.

Leaders of the movement sought to educate the black community, to build institutions, and to meet the daily needs of the people by providing protection, food, shelter, and clothing.[46] In addition, black power advocates much preferred the use of aggressive tactics to win the struggle for black freedom instead of the nonviolent resistance that was the hallmark of the SCLC civil disobedience protests and the SNCC sit-ins.

The militant message, calling for revolution by any means necessary, was more generously received by urban audiences in northern cities, who dealt with subtler, more veiled forms of racism and discrimination, than by activists in the South, who lived in fear of the brutal retaliation of white vigilantes for even perceived infractions of social customs.

Harsh rhetoric spewed from both sides in the SNCC debate about militant strategies versus nonviolent resistance tactics. Ella Baker argued against the radical redirection of SNCC and tried once again to mediate a dispute. However, a proposed retreat to deliberate about the issue and future direction of the organization overall never materialized. The ideological dispute divided

SNCC into opposing camps. In the end, the militant voices prevailed.

In the wake of the controversy, founding members John Lewis and Julian Bond resigned. Lewis explained that he was troubled by the open hostility to whites, along with what he felt was the diminishing relevance of SNCC programs. Bond was also disturbed by the ineffective programs and the constant ideological debates. Veteran field organizers began leaving. Diane Nash and James Lawson were replaced with more militant members. The old-guard founders of SNCC were pushed aside by the black power faction.

Baker served as director of the Washington, D.C., office of the Mississippi Freedom Democratic Party, started by Fannie Lou Hamer *(above). Credit:* Library of Congress

By 1967, the original SNCC organization was unrecognizable. Carmichael had become a nationally known figure, who dominated media coverage of SNCC and ruled from the top down. Militant black separatists also failed to cultivate grassroots leaders and even ridiculed poorly educated, stalwart freedom fighters like Fannie Lou Hamer in Mississippi. Ineffective programs led to a loss of northern financial backing. Adding to the financial troubles, other organizations began offering programs and competing for funds to support their efforts. The field operations deteriorated, and the quality of staff declined.

A new political reality also weakened SNCC, as well as the overall effectiveness of direct-action campaigns generally. Passage of the Civil Rights Act (1964) and Voting Rights Act (1965) armed blacks with the legal tools to fight discrimination in the courts rather than through sit-ins, marches, and street demonstrations. The attention of the nation turned to the turmoil of the free speech movement underway on the campus of the University of California at Berkeley during the 1964–1965 academic year. The peace movement in the late 1960s against the Vietnam War grabbed the headlines. Other protest movements diverted public attention away from the civil rights movement.

What was Ella Baker thinking during this tumultuous period? Increasingly, Baker anticipated a more radical form of social transformation through aggressive direct action. She well understood SNCC's impatience with the slow slog toward ending discrimination and righting social injustices. This annoyance with the status quo made the hard-line rhetoric and militant tactics of the black power movement attractive. Yet Baker found the move to exclude whites "counterproductive, misguided, and shortsighted."[47]

Although Baker's relationship with SNCC eroded as the black power advocates took control, she never severed her connection completely. She did, however, devote more time and energy to other projects and issues that concerned her. For a time, she served as director of the Washington, D.C., office of the Mississippi Freedom Democratic Party, started by Fannie Lou Hamer, and worked for the Southern Conference Education Fund (SCEF), even pushing for SCEF's involvement in the campaign to free Angela Davis from prison.[48]

Standing for Something

lla Baker passed on to others what was passed on to her. As she explained, since youth she had been tethered to a belief in Christian charity she learned from her parents and grandparents, from the teachings of the Baptist church, and from her schooling at Shaw Academy and University. She proudly claimed that she had been raised around "people who 'stood for something,' as I call it. Your relationship to human beings was more important than your relationship to the amount of money that you made."[49]

Rather than seeking high-paying jobs, Baker seized opportunities to build the skills of grassroots leaders, to establish organizational processes that would sustain locally grown programs, and to incorporate inclusiveness and consensus building in the governance of organizations.

Ella Baker in 1964. *Credit:* Photograph by Danny Lyon, Magnum Photos

Even in her declining years, when she had ceased working full time and was in poor health, Baker continued her advocacy for social justice causes. For example, she protested against the war in Vietnam, spoke on international women's rights, and backed the right for Puerto Rico to have full independence from the United States.

Since her death in New York in 1986, Ella Baker has been honored with the founding of the Ella Baker Center for Human Rights in Oakland, California, devoted to strengthening African American communities by giving people opportunities to work together. The Harlem branch library, later named the Schomburg Center for Research in Black Culture, established the Ella J. Baker Prize. The University of Virginia set up the Ella Baker

"Your relationship to human beings was more important than your relationship to the amount of money that you made."

Social Justice Award, given to a student organization working toward social justice for under-served, underrepresented, and disadvantaged populations. The Ella Baker/Septima Clark Human Rights Award, named after two exceptional civil rights activists, is bestowed by the American Educational Research Association.

Ella Baker's legacy lives on in these honors and awards, but a more lasting legacy is her transformative work of community organizing that secured freedom and justice for African Americans. Because her voice never wavered, she left an indelible footprint of daring courage and passionate commitment for others to follow. That is Baker's gift to future generations.

Ella Baker *(bottom)* with her adopted niece Jackie Brockington *(right)* and grandniece Carolyn Brockington *(left)*. *Credit:* Carolyn Brockington

Notes

1. Hear "Ella's Song" performed by Sweet Honey in the Rock online at the Ella Baker Center for Human Rights website, accessed August 24, 2016, http://ellabakercenter.org/blog/2013/12/ellas-song-we-who-believe-in-freedom-cannot-rest-until-it-comes.

2. *"Fundi: The Story of Ella Baker,"* Icarus Films, accessed July 23, 2016, http://icarusfilms.com/cat97/f-j/fundi45.html.

3. Faith S. Holsaert et al., eds., *Hands on the Freedom Plow: Personal Accounts by Women in SNCC* (Urbana: University of Illinois Press, 2010), 309.

4. Pat Aufderheide, quoted in *"Fundi: The Story of Ella Baker."*

5. Ella Baker, interview by Harry G. Boyte, January 15, 1977, quoted in Barbara Ransby, *Ella Baker and the Black Freedom Movement: A Radical Democratic Vision* (Chapel Hill: University of North Carolina Press, 2003), 39.

6. "Oral History Interview with Ella Baker, April 19, 1977," by Sue Thrasher and Casey Hayden, 20, interview G-0008, Southern Oral History Program Collection (#4007), *Documenting the American South,* University of North Carolina at Chapel Hill, 2007, http://docsouth.unc.edu/sohp/G-0008/G-0008.html.

7. "Interview with Baker" by Thrasher and Hayden, 2.

8. "Interview with Baker" by Thrasher and Hayden, 14.

9. "Interview with Baker" by Thrasher and Hayden, 14–15.

10. Ransby, *Ella Baker,* 32.

11. "Interview with Baker" by Thrasher and Hayden, 31.

12. Ransby, *Ella Baker,* 84.

13. Ransby, *Ella Baker,* 111.

14. Ransby, *Ella Baker,* 111.

15. Ransby, *Ella Baker,* 114–115.

16. Ransby, *Ella Baker,* 139.

17. Ransby, *Ella Baker,* 146.

18. Ransby, *Ella Baker,* 142.

19. Ransby, *Ella Baker,* 142–143.

20. Danielle L. McGuire, *At the Dark End of the Street: Black Women, Rape, and Resistance—A New History of the Civil Rights Movement from Rosa Parks to the Rise of Black Power* (New York: Alfred A. Knopf, 2010), xvii.

21. Ransby, *Ella Baker,* 162.

22. Ransby, *Ella Baker,* 173.

23. Taylor Branch, *Parting the Waters: America in the King Years*, 1954–1963 (New York: Simon and Schuster, 1989), 228–229, 232–234, 264.

24. Ransby, *Ella Baker,* 189.

25. Linda Brown, *Belles of Liberty: Gender, Bennett College, and the Civil Rights Movement in Greensboro, North Carolina* (Greensboro: Women and Wisdom Press, 2013), 77.

26. Anthony Lewis, *Portrait of a Decade: The Second American Revolution* (New York: Random House, 1964), 86.

27. "The Greensboro Chronology," International Civil Rights Center and Museum, accessed February 17, 2015, http://www.sitinmovement.org/history/greensboro-chronology.asp.

28. "Greensboro Chronology."

29. "Oral History Interview with Ella Baker, September 4, 1974," by Eugene Walker, 72, interview G-0007, Southern Oral History Program Collection (#4007), *Documenting the American South*, University of North Carolina at Chapel Hill, 2007, http://docsouth.unc.edu/sohp/G-0007/G-0007.html.

30. Branch, *Parting the Waters*, 557.

31. "Interview with Baker" by Walker, 66–68.

32. Clayborne Carson, *In Struggle: SNCC and the Black Awakening of the 1960s* (Cambridge, Mass.: Harvard University Press, 1995), 20.

33. Manning Marable and Leith Mullings, eds., *Let Nobody Turn Us Around: Voices of Resistance, Reform, and Renewal; An African American Anthology*, 2d ed. (New York: Rowman and Littlefield Publishers, 2009), 376.

34. "Jane Stembridge," *One Person, One Vote: The Legacy of SNCC and the Fight for Voting Rights*, SNCC Legacy Project and Duke University, accessed July 12, 2016, http://onevotesncc.org/profile/jane-stembridge/.

35. Marable and Mullings, *Let Nobody Turn Us Around*, 375.

36. Stephen Preskill, "*Fundi*: The Enduring Leadership Legacy of Civil Rights Activist Ella Baker," *Advancing Women in Leadership Online Journal* 18 (Spring 2005).

37. Holsaert et al., *Hands on the Freedom Plow*, 521.

38. John Lewis, interview, April 17, 1972, cited in Carson, *In Struggle*, 24.

39. Holsaert et al., *Hands on the Freedom Plow*, 308–309.

40. "*Fundi*: The Story of Ella Baker."

41. Carson, *In Struggle*, 41.

42. Holsaert et al., *Hands on the Freedom Plow*, 304.

43. Holsaert et al., *Hands on the Freedom Plow*, 304.

44. "A New Civil Rights Movement," *U.S. History: Pre-Columbian to the New Millennium*, USHistory.org, accessed July 11, 2016, http://www.ushistory.org/us/54i.asp.

45. Holsaert et al., *Hands on the Freedom Plow*, 534–535.

46. Judson L. Jeffries, "Black Power," *International Encyclopedia of the Social Sciences*, 2008, Encyclopedia.com, http://www.encyclopedia.com/topic/Black_power_movement.aspx.

47. Ransby, *Ella Baker*, 351.

48. Angela Y. Davis, a philosophy professor at the University of California, Los Angeles, member of the Communist Party, and supporter of the Black Panther Party, was indicted on charges of kidnapping, murder, and conspiracy in connection with the Marin County courthouse shoot-out by Jonathan Jackson to free Black Panther defendant James McClain on August 7, 1970. Davis was accused of purchasing the guns. Sol Stern, "The Campaign to Free Angela Davis and Ruchell Magee," June 27, 1971, *New York Times* online, https://www.nytimes.com/books/98/03/08/home/davis-campaign.html.

49. Ellen Cantarow, Susan Gushee O'Malley, and Sharon Hartman Strom, *Moving the Mountain: Women Working for Social Change* (Old Westbury, N.Y.: Feminist Press, 1979), 60.

Annotated Bibliography

Carson, Clayborne. *In Struggle: SNCC and the Black Awakening of the 1960s*. Cambridge, Mass.: Harvard University Press, 1995.

Records the full story of the Student Nonviolent Coordinating Committee (SNCC) and its cutting-edge role in the civil rights movement during the 1960s.

Charron, Katherine Mellen. *Freedom's Teacher: The Life of Septima Clark*. Chapel Hill: University of North Carolina Press, 2009.

Traces Clark's life from her earliest years to her evolution as an activist. Her gift to the civil rights movement was education. She developed a citizenship training program that enabled thousands of African Americans to register to vote.

Crawford, Vicki L., Jacqueline Anne Rouse, and Barbara Woods, eds. *Women in the Civil Rights Movement: Trailblazers and Torchbearers, 1941–1965*. Bloomington: Indiana University Press, 1990.

Presents individual women, including Ella Baker, who played essential roles in the civil rights movement and whose pioneering roles and contributions have often been overlooked and marginalized.

Feinstein, Stephen. *Inspiring African-American Civil Rights Leaders*. Berkeley Heights, N.J.: Enslow Publishers, 2013.

Chronicles the lives of eight civil rights leaders: W. E. B. DuBois, Philip Randolph, Martin Luther King Jr., James Farmer, Malcolm X, John Lewis, Fannie Lou Hamer, and Thurgood Marshall.

Grant, Joanne. *Ella Baker: Freedom Bound.* New York: John Wiley and Sons, 1998.

Explores the contributions of Ella Baker to the civil rights movement. Baker mentored, advised, and befriended a generation of young SNCC activists. She helped ordinary people soar to extraordinary heights.

Haskins, James. *One More River to Cross: The Stories of Twelve Black Americans.* New York: Scholastic Trade, 1992.

Presents brief biographies of twelve African Americans who courageously fought against racism to become leaders in their fields, including Marian Anderson, Ralph Bunche, Fannie Lou Hamer, and Malcolm X.

Holsaert, Faith S., Martha Prescod Norman Noonan, Judy Richardson, Betty Garman Robinson, Jean Smith Young, and Dorothy M. Zeller, eds. *Hands on the Freedom Plow: Personal Accounts by Women in SNCC.* Urbana: University of Illinois Press, 2010.

Captures the lives of an ethnically diverse group of fifty-two women, northern and southern, young and old, who share their courageous personal stories of working for SNCC on the front lines of the civil rights movement.

Kanefield, Teri. *The Girl from the Tar Paper School: Barbara Rose Johns and the Advent of the Civil Rights Movement.* New York: Abrams Books for Young Readers, 2014.

Tells the story of Barbara Rose Johns, a teenager who used nonviolent civil disobedience to lead a walkout at her racially segregated high school in 1951. The walkout drew attention to the unfair conditions in her school and was the first public protest of its kind. Johns grew up to become a librarian in the Philadelphia school system.

Marable, Manning, and Leith Mullings, eds. *Let Nobody Turn Us Around: Voices of Resistance, Reform, and Renewal; An African American Anthology.* 2d ed. New York: Rowman and Littlefield Publishers, 2009.

Compiles many voices in an anthology designed to acquaint readers with primary documents pertinent to African American history and the civil rights movement.

Mayer, Robert H. *When the Children Marched: The Birmingham Civil Rights Movement.* Berkeley Heights, N.J.: Enslow Publishers, 2008.

Discusses the Birmingham civil rights movement, the great leaders of the movement, and the role of the children who helped fight for equal rights and to end segregation in Birmingham.

McGuire, Danielle L. *At the Dark End of the Street: Black Women, Rape, and Resistance—A New History of the Civil Rights Movement from Rosa Parks to the Rise of Black Power.* New York: Alfred A. Knopf, 2010.

Describes the largely untold story of how the civil rights movement was, in part, started in protest against the rape of black women by white men who used sexual violence and terror to derail the freedom movement.

Payne, Charles M. *I've Got the Light of Freedom: The Organizing Tradition and the Mississippi Freedom Struggle.* Berkeley: University of California Press, 1995.

Examines the social struggle that drove the Mississippi civil rights movement and the everyday, nameless people who were inspired to change the conditions of their lives at great risk to their economic and physical survival. Ella Baker, Fannie Lou Hamer, and Septima Clark are included.

Ransby, Barbara. *Ella Baker and the Black Freedom Movement: A Radical Democratic Vision.* Chapel Hill: University of North Carolina Press, 2003.

Chronicles Baker's long and rich career as an organizer, an intellectual, and a teacher, from her early experiences in Depression-era Harlem to the civil rights movement of the 1950s and 1960s.

Williams, Lea E. "Dorothy Irene Height: A Life Well Lived." *Phi Kappa Phi FORUM* 91 (Summer 2011): 8–11.

Traces the remarkable life of Height from youth to adulthood, describing the people, places, and institutions that influenced her.

———. *Servants of the People: The 1960s Legacy of African American Leadership.* 2nd ed. New York: Palgrave Macmillan, 2009.

Profiles the lives of eight prominent leaders in the civil rights struggle, who embodied the qualities of servant leadership. Describes the repressive climate of racial hatred in America that spawned the movement and galvanized a generation of bold, persuasive leaders.

Index

About the Author

Lea E. Williams, an independent scholar in Greensboro, North Carolina, is a former administrator at Bennett College and North Carolina A&T State University. Currently she teaches English for Speakers of Other Languages (ESOL) at Guilford Technical Community College. Williams (www.leaewilliams.com) is the author of *Servants of the People: The 1960s Legacy of African American Leadership* (1996, rev. 2009), which profiles eight leaders in the civil rights movement.